P9-DTK-260

DATE DUE

BUSINESS SPAIN

A Practical Guide to Understanding Spanish Business Culture

Peggy Kenna   Sondra Lacy

Printed on recyclable paper

PASSPORT BOOKS
a division of *NTC Publishing Group*
Lincolnwood, Illinois USA

Library of Congress Cataloging-in-Publication Data

Kenna, Peggy.
   Business Spain: a practical guide to understanding Spanish
business culture / Peggy Kenna, Sondra Lacy.
       p.   cm.
   ISBN 0-8442-3563-6 (pbk.)
   1. Business etiquette—Spain.   2. Corporate culture—Spain.
   3. Business communication—Spain.   4. Negotiation in business—
Spain.   I. Lacy, Sondra.   II. Title.
HF5389.K458   1995
395' .52'0941—dc20   94-17746
                                                            CIP

Published by Passport Books, a division of NTC Publishing Group.
4255 West Touhy Avenue, Lincolnwood, (Chicago) Illinois 60646-1975, U.S.A.
©1995 by NTC Publishing Group. All rights reserved.
No part of this work may be reproduced, stored in a retrieval system
or transmitted in any form or by any means,
electronic or mechanical, including photocopying and recording or otherwise
without the prior permission of NTC Publishing Group.
Manufactured in the United States of America.

4 5 6 7 8 9 0 VP 9 8 7 6 5 4 3 2 1

Table of Contents

Peggy Kenna is a communications specialist working with foreign-born professionals in the American workplace. She provides cross-cultural training and consultation services to companies conducting business internationally. She is also a certified speech and language pathologist who specializes in accent modification. Peggy lives in Tempe, Arizona.

Sondra Lacy is a certified communications specialist and teaches American communication skills to foreign-born professionals in the American workplace. She also provides cross-cultural training and consultation services to companies conducting business internationally. Sondra lives in Scottsdale, Arizona.

Business Spain is an invaluable tool for thousands of entrepreneurs, businesspeople, corporate executives, technicians, and salespeople seeking to develop lasting business relationships in Spain.

The book provides a fast, easy way for you to become acquainted with business practices and protocol to help you increase your chances for success in Spain. You will discover the ˉrets of doing business internationally while improving your interpersonal communication skills.

Let this book work for you.

> Pam Del Duca
> President/CEO
> The DELSTAR Group
> Scottsdale, Arizona

Entrepreneur Of The Year®
Award Recipient

Business Spain offers a smooth and problem-free transition between the American and Spanish business cultures.

This pocket-size book contains information you need when traveling in Spain or doing business with Spanish colleagues. It explains the differences in business culture you will encounter in such areas as:

- Business etiquette

- Communication style

- Problem solving and decision making

- Meetings and presentation style

Business Spain gets you started on the right track and challenges you to seek ways to improve your success in the global marketplace by understanding cultural differences in the ways people communicate and do business with each other.

Successful international companies are able to adapt to the business styles acceptable in other countries and by other nationalities based on their knowledge and awareness of key cultural differences. These differences, if not acknowledged and addressed, can interfere in successful communication and can adversely affect the success of any business attempting to expand internationally.

Business Spain is designed to overcome such difficulties by comparing the American culture with the culture of Spain. Identifying appropriate behavior in one's own culture can make it easier to adapt to that of the country with which you are doing business. With this in mind, the book's unique parallel layout allows an at-a-glance comparison of Spanish business practices with those of the United States.

Practical and easy to use, *Business Spain* will help you win the confidence of Spanish associates and achieve common business goals.

The global business environment today is a multicultural one. While general business considerations are essentially the same the world over, business styles differ greatly from country to country. What is customary and appropriate in one country may be considered unusual or even offensive in another. The increasingly competitive environment calls for an individual approach to each national market. The success of your venture outside your home market depends largely upon preparation. The American style of business is not universally accepted. Yet we send our employees, executives, salespeople, technicians to negotiate or carry out contracts with little or no understanding of the cultural differences in the ways people communicate and do business with each other. How many business deals have been lost because of this cultural myopia?

Globalization is a process which is drawing people together from all nations of the world into a single community linked by the vast network of communication technologies. Technological breakthroughs in the past two decades have made instant communication between individuals around the world an affordable reality.

As these technological advances continue to open up and expand the dialogue among members of the world community, the need for effective communication between nations and peoples has accelerated.

When change occurs as dramatically and rapidly as we have witnessed in the past decade, many people throughout the world are being forced to quickly learn and adapt to unfamiliar ways of doing things. Some actually welcome change and the opportunities it presents, while others are reluctant to give up familiar ways of doing things. History proves that cultures are slow to change. But, individuals who are mentally prepared to accept change and deal with differences can successfully adapt to cultures very different from their own.

A culture develops when individuals have common experiences and share their reactions to these experiences by communicating with other members of their society.

Over time, communication becomes the vehicle by which cultural beliefs and values are developed, shared, and transmitted from one generation to the next. Communication and culture are mutually dependent.

Effective communication between governments or international businesses requires more than being able to speak the language fluently or relying on expert interpreters. Understanding the language is only the first step. Understanding and accepting the behaviors, customs, and attitudes of other cultures while interacting globally is also required to bring harmony and success in the worldwide business and political arena.

The importance of the influence of one's native culture on the way one approaches life cannot be overstated. Each country's cultural beliefs and values are reflected in its people's idea of the "right" way to live and behave.

In general, American businessmen and businesswomen who practice low-key, non-adversarial, win/win techniques in doing business abroad tend to be most successful. Knowing what your company wants to achieve — its bottom line — and also understanding the objectives of the other party and helping to accommodate them in the business transaction is necessary for developing long-term, international business relationships.

Often representatives from American companies have difficulty doing business with each other, even when they speak the same language and share a common culture. Consider how much more difficult it is to do business with people from different cultures who speak different languages.

Success in the international business arena will not be easy for Americans who do not take steps to gain the skills necessary to be a global player. The language barrier is an obvious problem..

Equally important will be negotiation skills, as well as an understanding of and adaptation to the social and business etiquette of the foreign country. Americans have a reputation for failing to appreciate this. In other words, American businessmen and businesswomen doing business abroad will get off to a good start if they remember to do the following:

- Listen closely; understand the verbal and non-verbal communications.
- Focus on mutual interests, not differences.
- Nurture long-term relationships.
- Emphasize quality. Be prepared to defend the quality of your products and services, and the quality of your business relationship.

Fast becoming a universal passport for doing business in Europe is ISO 9000. ISO stands for International Organization for Standardization.

There is a new set of concise standards covering documented quality control systems for product development, design, production, management, and inspection.

The European Economic Community (EEC) has adopted ISO certification and more than 20,000 European companies are complying. Increasing numbers of European companies are refusing to do business with foreign suppliers who don't meet ISO standards. Product areas under the most pressure to comply include automotive, aerospace, electronics, testing and measuring instruments, and products where safety and liability can become an issue. Companies with Total Quality Management (TQM) in place find it easier to pass ISO 9000 audits.

Successful companies will need to adapt to these rules and standards set by Europe in order to do business there.

Total Quality Management is becoming an integral part of successful companies in the United States.

TQM is an organized, company-wide effort to eliminate waste in every aspect of business and to produce the highest quality product possible. TQM is a philosophy that focuses on the customer, manages by facts, empowers people, and improves processes.

Implementation of the process is a real challenge and requires a company commitment to invest the time and finances necessary to reshape the entire organization. How is this accomplished? Through a team approach which values customer and employee opinions and in which everyone is committed to identify waste and its root cause and correct it in a timely manner. An effective tool for accomplishing this is through brainstorming efforts allowing everyone to participate. The successful TQM company is customer driven and uses leadership, information and analysis, strategic quality planning, human resource utilization, and quality assurance of products and services to reach goals.

Total Quality Management is a survival tool for businesses in a global market.

Spain was under a fascist dictatorship until the death of Francisco Franco in 1975 when King Juan Carlos took power. Since then, Spain has slowly been moving in the direction of a democracy.

Spain has been one of the poorest countries in Western Europe, although its economy has been steadily improving. During much of the 1980s, Spain had the highest GNP growth rate in Europe. It has since slowed somewhat and high unemployment has been a problem. The general recession in Western Europe, high unemployment and lower productivity, ethnic separatist movements and a high influx of refugees from North Africa have also been contributing factors in maintaining the economic growth of the 80s. One result has been a reasonably priced and skilled labor force available for people who want to do business there. Spain joined the Economic Community in 1986. The Olympic Games in Barcelona in 1992 were a major benefit to the economy of Spain and Catalonia particularly.

A major problem for the Spanish has been high unemployment and low productivity. There is also a large geographic imbalance in the distribution of wealth. Coupled with ethnic separatist movements and a high influx of refugees from North Africa, this has caused Spain to have difficulty in maintaining economic growth.

Industry has been expanding although agriculture and mining are important sectors of the economy. Spain has been slowly divesting key industries such as auto and oil from government ownership and putting more of the economy into the private sector. They also actively seek foreign investment in order to build their economy. Spain is a leading wine producer. Spanish farmers have been very hard hit by drought and water quality problems.

The region of Catalonia is in the extreme northeast of Spain and its capitol is Barcelona. Barcelona is very cosmopolitan and has close ties to France. This is the area of the biggest wine producers in Spain. Natives of Catalonia and natives of the rest of Spain, who claim Madrid as their capital, do not approve of each other and there is contention and rivalry between the two cities. Most Catalonians do not have Spanish-sounding names.

Catalonia is one of the most prosperous regions of Spain and has a high standard of living, which is reflected in the price of food, clothing, and consumer goods. Twenty-five percent of Spain's industry is located here, particularly textile, chemical, and mechanical equipment. Thirty-five percent of the population is engaged in industry, sixty percent in services, and five percent in agriculture such as grapes, apples, and pears.

Many women in Spain, especially in the larger cities of Madrid and Barcelona, are very career-oriented and successful in business. Social and educational status in large part determines the role of women in business. There are many women lawyers, doctors, scientists, and executives in retail businesses, especially fashion. U.S. businesswomen may find some macho attitudes but, in general, they will not have problems working with the Spanish business community.

There are five major languages spoken: Spanish, Catalan, Basque, Gallego, and Portuguese. Spanish is spoken by all but is considered a second language by one-fourth of the population who use their regional language for daily communication. Under Franco, only Spanish was allowed to be taught, spoken, or written. Since his death, all language restrictions have been removed. Most people in business will appreciate it if the foreigner attempts to speak to them in Spanish. They do not expect foreigners to speak their regional language.

The Spanish government is known for its huge bureaucracy. It is actually easier to open a business in Spain than to get a work permit there. They also like to help young entrepreneurs who want to open a new business.

Spain also has a large underground economy.

Prime Minister Felipe Gonzales Marquez will probably be in power through 1999. There have been long-term economic problems, tensions over immigrant workers, but he is moving from a socialist to a centrist position supported by his party and the regional parties. This current government began and is continuing with a successful fight against inflation.

IMPORTANT: Remember that within a culture, there are still individual differences among people and within business organizations.

United States

■ *Prone to overstatement*

Although Americans want to downplay the emotional aspects of business, they tend to be outgoing and, especially in sales, like to embellish or boast about their accomplishments, their company and its products and services. Today many businesses are starting to be conducted more on the reliability and integrity of a company and its products.

■ *Direct*

Americans like to state their purpose right away and want to get right down to business (get to the point). Timelines are very important.

Americans use small talk for developing rapport in order to work together more effectively. They are more comfortable meeting strangers and use small talk to get to know someone.

■ *Style*

Americans use self control and like to be perceived in their business communication as moderate and somewhat conservative.

■ *Understated*

While Spaniards are very warm and gregarious people and love to talk, they will understate their achievements. Personal pride and honor are very important to them, but they do not respect people who do a lot of bragging and boasting about themselves or their achievements.

■ *Indirect*

The Spanish usually don't come to the point right away. They expect this listener to read between the lines and figure out what they mean. The Spanish like to use small talk while doing business.

If they digress from the business conversation, they will become annoyed if you try to bring the discussion back to business before they are ready. Let them take the lead.

■ *Dramatic Style*

The Spanish can be dramatic and very animated in their conversation. They like to use superlatives. They tend to be eager and excitable and thus interrupt often. This is not meant to be rude but is considered a sign of interest.

United States

■ *Face saving less important*

To Americans accuracy is important but errors are tolerated. Admitting mistakes is seen as a sign of maturity. They believe you learn from failure and therefore encourage taking risks.

Americans believe criticism can and should be objective and impersonal (criticism of one's person is different from criticism of one's actions). However, all criticism should be done with tact.

■ *Gather facts*

Americans assume there are "facts" of life, of nature, of the universe that can be discovered by trained researchers. The most reliable facts, in the American view, are those in the form of quantities — specific numbers, percentages, rates, rankings, or amounts. Citing quantifiable facts is generally considered the best way to prove a point.

Americans tend to distrust intuition or any use of emotion when making decisions.

■ *Face saving important*

Criticism is seen as an exercise of rank and not a constructive piece of feedback. It is seen as personal and not objective.

To Spaniards, honor is very important. Spaniards tend to be very proud and find it very easy to perceive slights even when none is intended. They place great stress on personal honor, courtesy, and consideration.

■ *Value intuition and experience*

Spaniards are very practical when gathering information; however, they often tend to see gathering facts and data as a waste of time. They prefer to talk to people they trust and base decisions on intuition and experience.

United States

■ *Decision making*

One person is usually given power to make the final decision and bear all responsibility. Decisions tend to go from the top down. However, decision makers are found at all levels depending on the importance of the decision. Lower levels often get a chance to provide input. Americans believe that those closest to a problem should have input in determining the solution.

■ *Loyalty to self*

Lifetime loyalty to a company is no longer considered a major virtue; Americans' loyalty is to self and career.

In American companies, relationships can cross the boundaries of rank and seniority. Americans have a fundamental belief in the basic equality of all people. However, they do not always put this belief into practice.

■ *Decision making*

Family ownership has been common in Spain for decades. These ownership structures are complicated and sometimes you think you are dealing with the decision maker when you aren't.

Decision making can be rather slow since it is only done at the top and is a result of intuition rather than facts and statistics. These considerations often supplant material or technical advantages. Decisions are often based on personal relationships. Sharing decision making is seen as a weakness. Since decisions are made at the top, the problem is in getting managers to commit to implementing it. It is a good idea to cater to the decision makers.

■ *Loyalty to people not institutions*

Authority is determined by the quality of personal relationships with subordinates. An ideal leader is seen as a benevolent autocrat who is courageous but does not share decision making. Spanish managers are empire — not organization — builders.

Authority is based on trust and Spaniards feel the people most likely to be trusted are friends and family.

United States

■ *Schedule management*

Top businesspeople depend on their executive secretaries to keep their calendars and appointments although some like to set their own personal day schedule overlaying the business schedule.

Business days start as early as 7:30 or 8:00 AM and end around 5:00 PM. Lunch is usually one hour.

■ *Schedule management*

Top businesspeople handle their own calendars and their assistants may not know when and where they can be reached. They tend to make appointments for mornings and sometimes afternoons if the business is very important, but tradition is that afternoons are reserved for lunch and siesta.

Everything is usually closed from 2:00 to 4:00 PM daily except for restaurants. Businesses reopen from 5:00 to 8:00 PM.

United States

■ *Believe in change*

Americans believe change is good, but constant change causes established hierarchies and relationships to be repeatedly disrupted. The needs of the individual are subsidiary to the organization. Loyalty between employee and company is often temporary but expected to be wholehearted while it lasts.

■ *Staffing*

In America the relatives of company officers and managers often are barred from being hired. Nepotism is frowned upon in public companies where it is believed that promotions should be based on performance. It is more acceptable in family-owned companies. Generally employees are motivated to excel at their work by personal ambition.

Spain

■ *Centralized and hierarchical*

Business in Spain tends to be highly compartmentalized, bureaucratic, and centralized. There is little sense of collegiality; working relationships are essentially vertical. The heirarchy is very important.

■ *Staffing*

Family relationships are important in business. Trust and compatibility are what will secure the business relationship. Everyone should be treated with great respect.

The Spanish have a non-technical approach to business.

Spaniards prefer familiar faces they can trust. Nepotism is common. The family is the pillar of society. They feel more secure employing family and friends. The atmosphere in offices tends to be easygoing and friendly.

United States

■ *Planning*

Americans tend to be both strategic and tactical planners. Business contracts are written, detailed, and not very flexible. Any changes need to be renegotiated.

Planning tends to be fairly short term.

All mission statements and goal setting is envisioned at the top and communicated downward. Americans are constantly trying to predict the future.

■ *Think big*

Americans usually want to start with a major business transaction, a large contract. Business relationships are not personal and rarely become long-term relationships or commitments.

■ *Planning*

The Spanish are not very good at forecasting and planning since they have a very much "live for today" attitude and are not future oriented. They worry little about tomorrow.

Planning tends to be intuitive by the chief executive and is often not communicated downward. As a result there is often an atmosphere of crisis and emergency.

■ *Start small and build up*

Spaniards think in smaller units. They usually like to start a business relationship with a small transaction. Then, as trust is built and the relationship is developed, they will expand their business dealings.. They prize long-term relationships and the promise of long-term commitments.

United States

■ *Directive management*

In American companies someone is always in charge and there is a clear decision maker. Americans have little concept of shared responsibility. Whoever is put in charge of implementing a decision is expected to be completely accountable for its success or failure.

Americans are procedures oriented and like to outline exactly what is to be done. They believe that relationships only need to be established at the level of the decision maker.

■ *Management*

Business in Spain tends to be highly compartmentalized, bureaucratic, and authoritarian. An effort is being made by younger managers to implement many American methods of management.

It is not always possible to get access to the decision maker. It may be necessary to work through and help the person you built the relationship with to persuade the decision maker.

United States

■ *Time is money*

Americans are very bound by time. They feel that once a moment is gone it is gone forever, therefore letting time go by without "doing" something is like wasting money. They also like to divide a day into segments and schedule each segment. Punctuality is very important. Americans are also very future oriented.

■ *Fast pace*

Americans want to get down to business right away. They tend to establish relationships quickly and the relationship is usually only temporary until business is completed.

Business is usually done during work hours: 8:00 AM to 5:00 PM.

■ *Time is fluid*

A 15-20 minute wait is very common. If it gets much longer, it might mean the other person got tied up somewhere else or it might mean they aren't very interested in your proposal.

The concept of time has changed dramatically in Spain. They no longer have a "mañana" attitude. However, the Spanish wish to enjoy the present and may forget appointments made several days previously. But if they have an important stake in the business, appointments will be kept. They are not future oriented.

■ *Slower pace*

They try to do many things at once, which can result in much procrastination and delay. The Spanish tend to view the present as tenuous and insecure and are not future oriented. Much business is conducted over the evening meal, which seldom starts before 9:00 PM. And no one is in a hurry.

Although the Spanish have a tradition of hospitality and take pleasure in unhurried conversation, decisions can be made very quickly and they generally stick to implementation schedules.

United States

■ *Very schedule oriented.*

Meeting deadlines and commitments is very important to Americans and everything is scheduled. Americans management and workers both try very hard to meet these schedules

■ *Dislike schedules*

Delivery dates are not to be taken literally. Imposing detailed schedules and quality checks can be resented. It is not uncommon to find sudden changes of plan, being completely stood up with no excuses offered, or business meetings dragging on so long you are late for your next appointment. They have a much more relaxed and mellow attitude toward schedules.

United States

■ *Communication tool*

Some meetings are brainstorming for ideas; some are to disseminate information; some are to persuade or discuss, defend, and decide.

Americans like to get down to business right away since meetings are usually tightly scheduled and have a fixed agenda. A meeting may be adjourned before all business is completed. Americans also always like to leave with some kind of action plan.

There are formal and informal meetings. Informal meetings can become very heated with a number of confrontations and disagreements to be resolved, or can be just for brainstorming. Formal meetings have a leader, an agenda, and everyone is polite.

■ *Communicate instructions*

Spain is not a formal meetings culture. The purpose of many meetings is to communicate instructions. Collaboration is seen more as voicing opinions than arriving at decisions or especially at implementing them. It is best to get a consensus to get something accomplished; to do this, meeting leaders try to get attendees to agree with them (the leader) rather than with each other. In business the Spanish tend to be analytical and contemplative.

Informal meetings can be frequent and are likely to be rather noisy with everyone talking at once and apparently not listening. They constantly interrupt each other. A speaker must be very determined to get a point across. If the discussion wanders, it is best to wait until the leaders are ready to bring the discussion back to business.

The Spanish like to conduct business over a meal — many important decisions are made here. Spaniards tend to loosen up in informal surroundings such as a restaurant. Such meetings are usually very impromptu and you are expected to drop everything and go. Sometimes meetings can seem to be about personal matters.

Initial business meetings may be very casual. It is best to let them bring up business at their own pace.

United States

■ *Presentations*

Americans tend to have a projecting style of presentation. They often combine informative and persuasive styles as an efficient method of presentation. They attempt to persuade the audience to make a decision or take an action at the same time as they provide information. They consider this an effective and efficient use of time. Americans also believe in the "hard sell" and "quick close" approach to selling. They expect the audience to ask questions and to test the presenter's knowledge. Presenters expect to defend their opinions.

■ *Presentations*

The Spanish like speakers who are very eloquent. Joking is inappropriate. It is a good idea to center on tangibles such as samples, visuals, etc.

Be forceful and clear. Emphasize stability. Don't expect immediate conclusions or results.

Make your proposals detailed and practical. They believe that a good presentation can be eloquent and formal yet forceful and clear. It should center on tangibles with visuals, product demonstrations, and explanations that are detailed and practical.

It is unlikely that conclusions or results or decisions will be made during the meeting.

United States

■ *Task oriented*

Americans are highly task oriented. They are good at taking responsibility and getting things done. They are more interested in the technical aspects of negotiation than in building relationships.

Americans tend to make concessions grudgingly at all times. They are not hagglers. Americans usually bargain for clear-cut goals such as price, quality, or delivery date.

■ *Direct and open*

Americans are also very open and direct in their communication. They like to deal with differences directly. They also tend to be rather poor listeners and have a tendency to interrupt.

■ *Appeal to logic*

Presentations during negotiations are usually fairly formal and Americans like appeals to logic rather than emotion. They are principally concerned with marketing projections and strategies.

■ *Relationship oriented*

The Spanish expect to establish a solid relationship. Trust, rapport, and compatibility are essential to doing business in Spain. If you can do someone a personal favor you will have a friend and ally for life.

Spaniards don't do much bargaining; they believe they sell at an honest and fair price so there is no need to bargain. They do not pay a lot of attention to detail.

■ *Honor important*

Pride and honor are very important to the Spanish. They do not like to be embarrassed.

Modesty is valued over assertiveness.

■ *Concerned with price*

Many Spaniards have been educated in the U.S. and, like many Europeans, are acculturated to the protocol of American negotiating.

The major concern of the Spanish when negotiating is price, not technical details. Grandiose schemes are not likely to be well accepted.

United States

■ *Impatient*

Decisions are often made quickly. Not all decisions need to be made by executives; sometimes lower-level managers can make decisions. Sometimes their impatience to complete negotiations can lead Americans to make unnecessary concessions.

Punctuality is important. Americans will seldom be more than a few minutes late to a meeting or negotiating session. They expect others to be equally punctual. They also like agendas for negotiating sessions and expect these agendas to be adhered to.

■ *Contracts*

Americans are legalistic and like detailed contracts with all contingencies spelled out. These contracts tend to be fairly inflexible and are expected to be adhered to.

■ *Slower paced*

The pace of negotiations is usually slow and relaxed. Don't push. They believe in taking their time to make decisions.

Although they seldom abide by an agenda, the Spanish like to have one to start a meeting with.

■ *Agreement*

If a meeting concludes with "We'll let you know," it may mean the decision maker wasn't there or it may mean they aren't interested. The Spanish don't like to say "no" directly.

Agreements usually start with an oral agreement indicated by a handshake. This is then followed by a written document. Contracts entered into will be strictly fulfilled by the Spanish and they expect the same.

U.S. Business Etiquette

- Be punctual. Americans are very time conscious. They also tend to conduct business at a fairly fast pace.

- A firm handshake and direct eye contact is the standard greeting.

- Direct eye contact is very important in business. Not making eye contact implies boredom or disinterest.

- Gift giving is not common. The United States has bribery laws which restrict the value of gifts which can be given.

- The United States is not particularly rank and status conscious. Titles are not used when addressing executives. Americans usually like to use first names very quickly. Informality tends to be equated with equality.

- Business meetings usually start with a formal agenda and tasks to be accomplished. There is usually very little small talk. Participants are expected to express their ideas openly; disagreements are common.

- If there is no one to introduce you in a business meeting, you may introduce yourself and present your card.

- Permission should be asked before smoking.

- It is common to discuss business over breakfast, lunch, or dinner. Also, some business deals are still concluded on the golf course.

- Business dress is basically conservative but gets more informal the further west you go.

- Decision making is actually decentralized and dispersed among many individuals and groups. It is important to find out who has final authority. Decision making tends to be quick.

- Many women hold middle-management positions in the United States and a steadily growing number are in top executive positions. The same courtesy and respect should be shown women as men in business. Special or traditional courtesies such as opening doors are not always appreciated by women executives.

- U.S. companies pride themselves on being efficient, purposeful, direct, single-minded, and materialistic. The bottom line is very important.

- Titles — Señor, Señora, Señorita — are used with last names in business. The mother's family name is attached to a person's name in written communication (Señor Jose Martinez Lopez). So the middle name may be the surname (last name).

- Always use titles until the other person gives you permission to be more informal. Do not use first names unless asked to do so.

- The Spanish appreciate it if you learn a few words in Spanish, although they know that Americans are not traditionally good with languages. Let them know you are hoping to improve and learn their language better.

- When meeting a person for the first time, ask who they are, not what they do. It is generally safe to talk about children and sports.

- Service in restaurants is generally unhurried. Be prepared to be patient. Tipping is considered an insult.

- If you are invited to someone's home for dinner, it is considered an honor and a special occasion. You can bring a gift such as wine, flowers, cheese, etc.

- Dress well and speak with as much flair and eloquence as you can. Appearances are important. They appreciate an air of sophistication.

- Business is not conducted in the afternoon from 2:00 to 4:00.

- Don't be put off by occasional "advise giving" or "corrections." Spaniards often consider it their duty to correct "errors" by others.

- Spaniards are very formal. Shaking hands upon meeting and leaving is customary. Handshakes are warm and friendly and often accompanied by a light pat on the back.

- Courtesy is very important to the Spanish. They like formal greetings and politeness is very important..

- The Spanish engage in a lot of business socializing in order to establish relationships of trust. When introducing yourself tell who you are, where you come from, and what your business is.

- Americans tend to stand an arm's length away from each other.

- Americans generally respect queues or lines. To shove or push one's way into a line will often result in anger and verbal complaint.

- Beckoning is done by raising the index finger and curling it in and out, or by raising the hand and curling the fingers back toward the body.

- Using the hand and index finger to point at objects or to point directions is common.

- Whistling is a common way to get the attention of someone at a distance.

- "No" is signalled by waving the forearm and hand (palm out) in front and across the upper body, back and forth.

- Americans use the standard "OK" sign, the "V" for victory sign, and the thumbs-up sign.

- The closer the Spanish stand to you, the more they are indicating trust. Close friends often touch each other when conversing.

- Local residents often seem to push and shove when in line or pubic situations, since their space limits are closer than Americans'. But visitors are usually respected. They are also not as given to forming lines as Americans are.

- Eye contact is important but women should be wary of eye contact from strange men.

- The Spanish tend to use a lot of arm and head gestures. Hands should not be placed in the pockets when conversing since hands are used a lot in conversation.

- Shaking hands loosely means "I can't believe the person acted that way."

- The American "OK" sign is considered obscene.

- To beckon someone, stretch out the arm and hand, palm down, and make a scratching motion toward your body.

Communication Interferences

Effective communication, both verbal and nonverbal, means that the sending and processing of information between people, countries, and businesses is understood, examined, interpreted, and responded to in some way. Any factor that causes a barrier or eliminates the successful transmission of information is defined as a communication interference.

- **Environmental interference** is an actual physical disturbance in the environment such as power outage, unregulated temperatures, a person or group talking very loudly, etc.

- **Physiological interference** can be a hearing loss, laryngitis, illness, stuttering, neurological or organic deficit, etc.

- **Semantic interference.** We understand a word to have a certain meaning but the other person has a different meaning. Body language and gestures mean different things to different people. This includes confusion of abbreviated organizational jargon and pronunciation. Universal meanings (semantic understanding) are rare.

- **Syntactic interference.** Words are placed in certain order to give our language meaning. If the words are out of order, the meaning may be changed (this includes grammar).

- **Organizational interference.** Ideas being discussed lack sequence and can't be followed.

- **Psychological interference.** Words that incite emotion are used. In any emotional state (positive or negative) emotions need to be diffused in order to communicate effectively.

- **Social interference.** This includes cultural manners that are inappropriate for the country, such as accepted codes for dress, business etiquette, communication rules, social activity.

Always become well informed about the customs and culture and get information before you try and do business in another country. Review this book and decide which areas of communication you and your colleagues will have difficulty with in Spain. Anticipate and plan accordingly.

As the visitor to another country, you need to move out of your "comfort zone." Make the people from another country feel comfortable doing business with you.

No one country has a lock on world markets. Fundamental changes have occurred in the world economy in the last decade. New technologies and low labor costs often give nations that once were not major players an advantage. This results in increased competition. Yet international business is vital to any country's prosperity.

Business is conducted by people, and the future of any country in a global economy will lie with people who can effectively think and act across ethnic, cultural, and language barriers. We need to understand that the differences between nations and cultures is profound. The European-based culture of the United States has very different values and behaviors than other cultures in the world. If you cannot accept and adapt to these differences, you will not succeed.

Companies striving to market their business overseas can become truly successful only when they recognize that the key is operating with sensitivity toward the culture and communication of the other country. Communication cannot be separated from culture and this is true when doing business in other countries.

No flourishing company would present themselves to another company in the same country without researching that company's business culture and then adapting their image to meet the customer's comfort level. It's the same when doing business in another country. You must adapt your image by using your knowledge of effective cultural communication to present a positive public image to the other country.

The first thing is to identify your target audience: clients, customers, suppliers, financial people, government employees, and so on. Then you must learn how to effectively communicate with them, and this means learning the culture.

Business failure internationally rarely results from technical or professional incompetence. It is often due to a lack of understanding of what people from other countries want, how they work, and so on. This lack of understanding can put a company at a tremendous disadvantage.

Learning the business protocol and practices of the country where you want to do business can give you great leverage. The more you know about the people you do business with, the more successful you can be. Businesspeople need to make every contact they have with a foreign customer or business partner a positive one. Business leaders and managers must rethink the way they do business in the new global marketplace.

Succeeding in International Business

To be successful in the global market, you must:

- **Be flexible.** Cultural adaptations are necessary for both countries to get along and do business. Resisting the local culture will only lead to distrust.

- **Be patient.** Adjust your planning. Initiating business in many countries takes a long-range approach and may require two or three years. Anticipate problems and develop alternative strategies.

- **Prepare thoroughly.** Research the country, the organization, the culture, and beliefs of the people you will be dealing with.

- **Know your bottom line.** Know exactly what you want from a deal and at what point an agreement is not in your best interest. Know when to walk away.

- **Form relationships.** Encourage getting involved with the new community if you're going to be in the country for a long period.

- **Keep your cool.** Pay attention to the wide range of national, cultural, religious, and social differences you encounter.

- **Show respect.** Search for the other side's needs and interests. Accentuate the positive. Don't preach your own beliefs and respect their beliefs.

When you are using this book, review your own beliefs and values about correct business protocol and ethics. Then match these ideas with the business practices and protocol in Spain.

You can contribute to your own success by recognizing that you will have to move out of your own "comfort zone" of doing business into the cultural business zone of Spain in order to develop the rapport necessary to meet the needs of your client or partner. This does not mean you compromise your company's image or product but that you do business following Spain's protocol while there. It's only for a short time that you may be following their rules, and the payoff can be one in which concepts can be sold while still maintaining a consistent image and approach that is culturally appropriate.

- The United States is a very ethnically diverse country. To do business, it is important to be open to this diversity and to be flexible.

- Americans tend to be very individually oriented and concerned with their own careers. Their first loyalty is to themselves.

- Americans want to be liked. They prefer people who are good team players and want to cooperate.

- Americans value equality and dislike people who are too status or rank conscious.

- Most Americans are open, friendly, casual, and informal in their manners. They like to call people by their first name quickly.

- Americans like to come right to the point and are uncomfortable with people who are indirect and subtle. They like a direct and specific "yes" or "no."

- Americans expect people to speak up and give their opinions freely and to be honest in the information they give.

- Americans can be very persistent. When they conclude a business transaction and sign a contract, they expect it to be honored. They do not like people who change their minds later.

■ Research local economic trends. Also do your research on how to reach the Spanish customer. People don't tend to advertise in newspapers or yellow pages, but use public promotions, flyers, contests, etc.

■ Have a good local introduction. You are actually better off getting a Spanish partner if you want to do business there. Madrid and Barcelona are the two major locations for business enterprise. Barcelona is much more like western Europe.

■ Use an interpreter or translator who knows the regional language. You can hire one yourself or use one of your Spanish counterparts. Learn some Spanish yourself and perhaps some of the regional language.

■ Be prepared to work late. Spanish businesses usually close for several hours in the afternoon and then work late into the evening.

■ Learn about local politics.

Common Phrases

Although Spanish is the common language, it is spoken as a second language by a large percentage of the population. Catalan is spoken by many Spaniards.

English	Spanish	Catalan
Good morning	Buenos días	Bon dia
Good afternoon	Buenas tardes	Bona tarda
Good evening	Buenas noches	
Please	Por favor	Si us plau
Thank you	Gracias	Gracie
You're welcome	De nada	De res
Goodbye	Adiós	Adeu
My name is ...	Me llamo ...	
What's your name?	Cómo te llamas	
Pleased to meet you	Mucho gusto	
How are you?	Cómo está	
Fine, thank you	Bien, gracias. Y usted?	
Yes/No	Sí/No	
Mr/Mrs/Miss	Señor/Señora/Señorita	
See you again	Hasta pronto/ Hasta mañana	

Notes

Available in this series:

For more information, please contact:

Sales and Marketing Department
NTC Publishing Group
4255 West Touhy Avenue
Lincolnwood, IL 60646
798-679-5500